Making Sense of Dollar$ and Cent$

Karen E. Burks

Hello There!

Meet your Financial Literacy friends Christine Coin, Donovan Dollar, and Rhonda Rich. They will be your guide to complete the activity and coloring book. Let's get started!!

A E G S L O A N C T V U V T E N O K J O L S
X B Q R T Z D N M K H J L E A R W I R F F L
F I W X C V S H F C O D Y H P W D H W U G G
Y T C K M S E L Q A M T G B C R N V G K P A
E C U I R H R G P S O A D O S A F G N L E I
J A O U Y R G D L H A X Z D V U O U J J S N
O R X N W X K N F C N E A P G A I T N O K B
B D V D C R E D I T X S P U N H L D S L M H
D T V H Q D P A G C B F W F O M E U Q F F O
R E S I N T E R E S T E N K Q C D R E O M M
Z W F Y F X J U I R R J O C E J F P I T U B
C G K R N L B P M L M V Z N F X G L R I S K
X W F T E A C C O U N T I T J S T J P U R S
T P E V Q O Y F M B H O H P D O M V Q N W D
M O N E Y N I D F Y C R B Q B U D G E T L Y
W I R H M E E S A R E E K S V H V N X Q X I
U B V A D L B E G U W Y A E Q V F E W R Q P
Y S H K Y J A S C A P I T A L Z S H U S Z T
Q D O L L A R X E S R Z Y J D C O S T I R C
S G Z L V C H A R G E A E L T E Z Y V A M R

BANK	BUDGET	CASH	DEBIT CARD
LOAN	RISK	CREDIT	VALUE
MONEY	ACCOUNT	WORK	GAIN
DOLLAR	COIN	RATE	INTEREST
CHARGE	CAPITAL	PROFIT	COST

Complete the deposit slip for $45 cash and a $20 check. Be sure to bring the check and deposit slip with you to the bank on the next page.

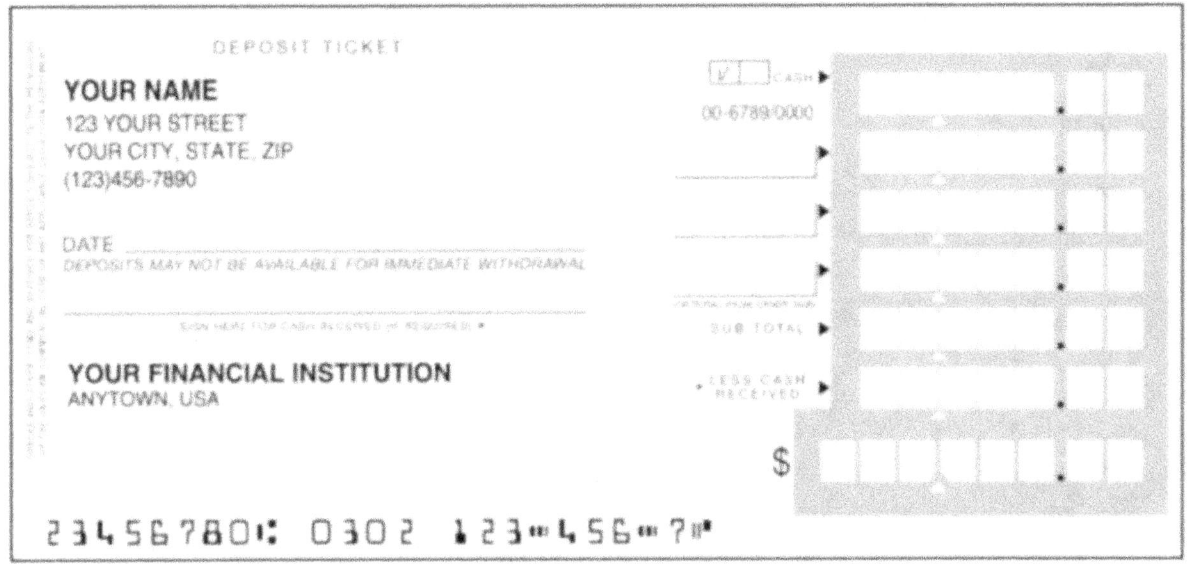

1. Fill in the date

2. List the cash amount of your deposit

3. List the check amount (if any) along with the check numbers

4. If you are depositing money but want some of the cashback, list the amount of cashback in the Less Cash Received section

5. Add up deposits for a subtotal.

Follow the steps Christine Coin provides to fill out this check for $93.21

1. Write the date

2. Put down the recipients name

3. Fill in the dollar amount

4. Spell out the dollar amount

5. Complete the memo line

6. Sign the check

BANK
BANK

ABC's of Currency

Fill in the missing letter and find the definition

Annual __ercentage rate -

Bud__et -

Curren_y -

Debt to I_come -

E_onomy -

Finan_e -

G_ld -

Household In_ome -

I_terest Rate -

J_int Account -

K_d Bank Account -

Lo_n -

Mor_gage -

N_t Income -

Over_raft -

P_ofit -

Qu_lity Control -

Resi_ual -

Sto_ks/Sh_res -

Ta_es -

U_ilities -

Val_e -

With_rawl -

X r_te -

Y_eld -

Zer_ Balance Ac_ount -

Add each pair of currency together. Then
tell how much money there is all together
on the page.

10¢

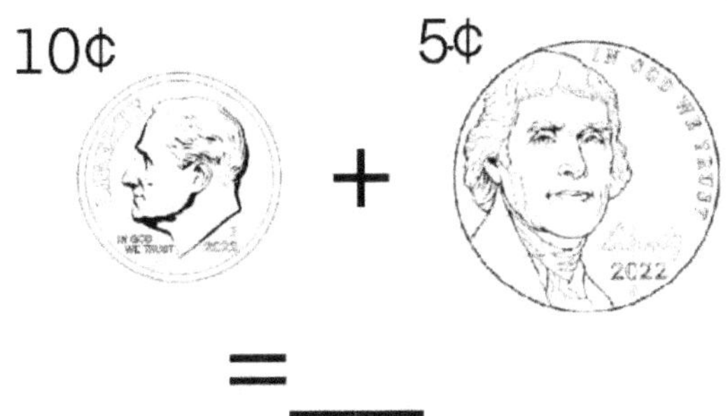

5¢

=

___

1¢

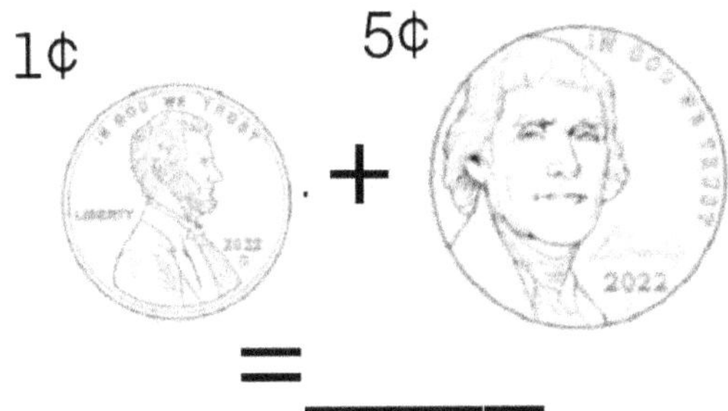

5¢

=

___

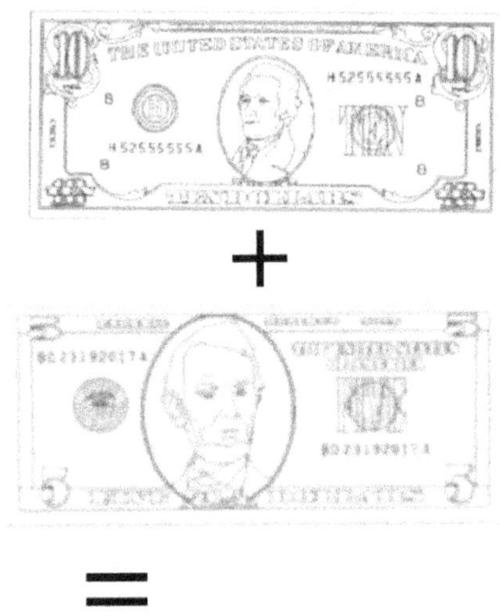

=

___

10¢

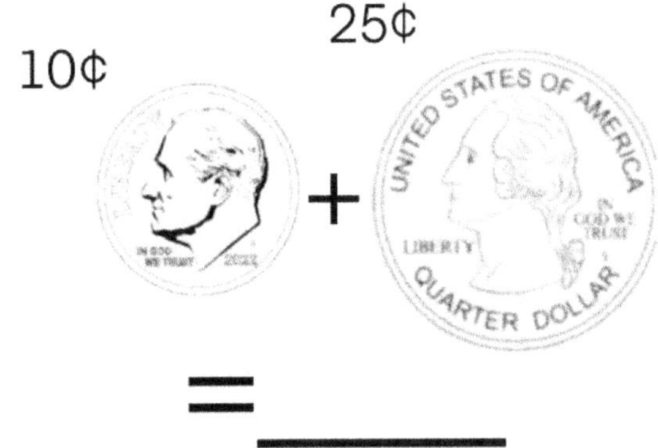

25¢

=

___

=

___

=

___

Let's get our money into shape. Match the financial shapes and terms.

Dollar
(rectangle)

Coin
(circle)

Piggy Bank
(oval)

Money Vault
(square)

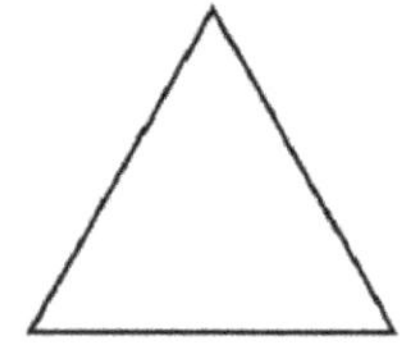

Gold Block
(trapezoid)

Bank
(pentgon)

Triangle

Use this page to create a savings goal. List the date and amount of each deposit. Color in the bank as you reach your goal

I'm saving for

_______________________________________.

Date   Amount

___ ___

I need to save $__________

___ ___

___ ___

___ ___

1/3 of the way there   2/3 of the way there   3/3 GOAL REACHED!

___ ___

___ ___

___ ___

___ ___

<h1 style="text-align:center">Define the following Money Terms</h1>

Bank-

Loan-

Charge-

Budget-

Risk-

Account-

Coin-

Capital-

Cash-

Credit-

Work-

Rate-

Profit-

Debit Card-

Value-

Gain-

Interest-

Cost-

Making Sense of Dollar$ and Cent$
Certificate of Completion

This certificate is awarded to:

Recognition for achieving their successful completion of the
"Making Sense of Dollar$ and Cent$ coloring and activity book
on the _______ day of the month of _____________________ in the
year of __________

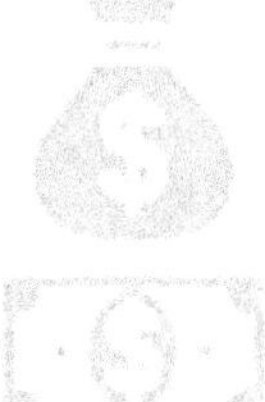

About The Author

Karen serves as the Founder of Burks Management Firm, a consulting firm where she assists clients with financial education training, workforce development, and business consulting. She has over a decade of expertise in the financial institution industry and five years in workforce development implementation. Karen also serves as the Economic Empowerment Director at her church United Christian Faith Ministries and Southeastern Louisiana University Upward Bound Personal Finance Instructor.

Karen's Favorite Finance Quote:
"An investment in knowledge pays the best interest." -Benjamin Franklin

This activity coloring book is a financial literacy education support for young scholars. It's designed to cultivate the financial fundamentals in a creative and interactive way.

Learn more about her work at www.burksmgmtfirm.com

Notes